SPORTS INJURIES:
HOW TO PREVENT, DIAGNOSE, & TREAT

WEIGHT TRAINING

Sports Injuries:
How to Prevent, Diagnose, & Treat

- Baseball
- Basketball
- Cheerleading
- Equestrian
- Extreme Sports
- Field
- Field Hockey
- Football
- Gymnastics
- Hockey
- Ice Skating
- Lacrosse
- Soccer
- Track
- Volleyball
- Weight Training
- Wrestling

SPORTS INJURIES:
HOW TO PREVENT, DIAGNOSE, & TREAT

WEIGHT TRAINING

CHRIS McNAB

MASON CREST PUBLISHERS
www.masoncrest.com

Mason Crest Publishers Inc.
370 Reed Road
Broomall, PA 19008
(866) MCP-BOOK (toll free)
www.masoncrest.com

First printing

1 2 3 4 5 6 7 8 9 10

Library of Congress Cataloging-in-Publication Data on file
at the Library of Congress

ISBN 1-59084-641-9

Series ISBN 1-59084-625-7

Editorial and design by
Amber Books Ltd.
Bradley's Close
74–77 White Lion Street
London N1 9PF
www.amberbooks.co.uk

Project Editor: Michael Spilling
Design: Graham Curd
Picture Research: Natasha Jones

Printed and bound in the Hashemite Kingdom of Jordan

PICTURE CREDITS
Corbis: 6, 8, 11, 12, 14, 16, 18, 20, 22, 24, 26, 32, 35, 37, 40, 42, 54, 56, 58, 59; **©EMPICS**: 41; **Topham Picturepoint**: 15.

FRONT COVER: All Corbis.

ILLUSTRATIONS: Courtesy of Amber Books except:
Bright Star Publishing plc: 46, 51, 52;
Tony Randell: 49.

IMPORTANT NOTICE
This book is intended to provide general information about sports injuries, their prevention, and their treatment. The information contained herein is not intended as a substitute for professional medical care. Always consult a doctor before beginning any exercise program, and for diagnosis and treatment of any injury. Accordingly, the publisher cannot accept any responsibility for any prosecution or proceedings brought or instituted against any person or body as a result of the use or misuse of the techniques and information within.

CONTENTS

Foreword

Sports Injuries: How to Prevent, Diagnose, and Treat is a seventeen-volume series written for young people who are interested in learning about various sports and how to participate in them safely. Each volume examines the history of the sport and the rules of play; it also acts as a guide for prevention and treatment of injuries, and includes instruction on stretching, warming up, and strength training, all of which can help players avoid the most common musculoskeletal injuries. *Sports Injuries* offers ways for readers to improve their performance and gain more enjoyment from playing sports, and young athletes will find these volumes informative and helpful in their pursuit of excellence.

Sports medicine professionals assigned to a sport that they are not familiar with can also benefit from this series. For example, a football athletic trainer may need to provide medical care for a local gymnastics meet. Although the emergency medical principles and action plan would remain the same, the athletic trainer could provide better care for the gymnasts after reading a simple overview of the principles of gymnastics in *Sports Injuries*.

Although these books offer an overview, they are not intended to be comprehensive in the recognition and management of sports injuries. The text helps the reader appreciate and gain awareness of the common injuries possible during participation in sports. Reference material and directed readings are provided for those who want to delve further into the subject.

Written in a direct and easily accessible style, *Sports Injuries* is an enjoyable series that will help young people learn about sports and sports medicine.

Susan Saliba, Ph.D., National Athletic Trainers' Association Education Council

A woman tones her shoulder and arm muscles. Weight training is now popular among women as well as men.

The Basics of Weight Training

Weight training is the precise development of muscles using resistance exercises, freeweights, or weight machines. Over the past thirty years, it has become one of the most popular forms of exercise in the world.

Weight training is popular for good reasons. Not only does it make you feel strong and improve your health, but it also makes you look slimmer and more toned and athletic. Looking good is important to some, but this should not be the main reason you take up weight training. Concentrating only on appearance may make you push your training forward faster than your body allows. That is when injuries happen. Instead, concentrate on weight training's clear health benefits:

- It builds up muscle strength, making muscles and joints less vulnerable to injury and disease, particularly in later life.
- When combined with a proper diet, it helps you to lose weight. Each pound of muscle burns up thirty to forty calories a day. The more muscle you have, the more fat you lose.
- Weight training is a great way to control stress. It releases "feel good" chemicals in your body, called **endorphins**, which give you a sense of well-being.

A weightlifter steps up to the bar. Professional weightlifters can lift more than double their own body weight. The effort can push their heart rate to around 200 beats a minute.

- It can make you physically stronger and more capable of safely handling heavy loads.
- It will help you to perform better in other sports, boosting **aerobic** fitness and muscular power.

All are excellent reasons to begin weight training. So how does weight training work?

MUSCLE DEVELOPMENT

In your body, there are more than 600 muscles. Each muscle is built up of tiny fibers called myofibrils. When we need to perform a task requiring muscle power, our brain sends electrical orders to the muscle fibers via special nerve cells called neurons. The muscle fibers contract or expand according to these orders which they receive from the brain.

Weight training results in improved strength and muscle bulk for several different reasons. First, the myofibrils respond to the weight training by growing thicker and stronger. Second, the actual number of myofibrils increases, expanding the size and power of the muscle. Finally, weight training improves the communication between the brain and the muscles.

We acquire any skill through practice, and doing weight training makes us more familiar with our bodies, giving us the balance, strength, and focus needed to lift heavy objects. Indeed, for this reason alone, beginners at weight training develop additional strengths even before their muscles have started to grow.

Weight training does not necessarily require weights. Much good work can be done just through age-old techniques such as push-ups, **crunches**, and **triceps** dips. These have the big advantage that you can do them anywhere—living room, bedroom, or yard. Repeated every day in increasing numbers, such exercises will

A modern gymnasium. Each machine is configured to develop a particular muscle group. The machine in the foreground, for example, is used to strengthen hamstrings, quadriceps, and calf muscles.

result in a strong physique. The muscle development using weightless exercises, however, is generally neither as fast nor as comprehensive as training using weights.

OPTIONS FOR TRAINING

There are two systems of weights in strength training—**freeweights** or weight machines. Freeweights are simply heavy disks of metal (or, sometimes, weighted plastic), attached to a bar for lifting. There are generally two types of freeweights: a **dumbbell**, which is designed to be held in one hand; or a long **barbell**, which is held in both hands. Combined with an exercise bench—a long, narrow bench,

The humble dumbbell. Though the simplest of weights, dumbbells can be used to strengthen almost all muscle groups of the upper body, including abdominals and upper-back muscles.

where you can lie or sit while lifting—freeweights are sufficient for successful weight training.

Freeweights have their pros and cons. The pros are:

- a huge number of different exercises can be performed with the most basic set of freeweights;
- freeweights are excellent for isolating individual muscles so that other stronger muscle groups come to their aid;
- freeweights are far less expensive to buy than weight machines.

But the disadvantages of freeweights should not be overlooked:

- they are more difficult to use properly than weight machines because they require good balance. For this reason, you are more likely to injure yourself using freeweights if you have not been trained in the correct technique;
- doing freeweights on your own can be dangerous—you run the risk of dropping them on yourself.

The alternative to freeweights is weight machines. Weight machines are pieces of equipment scientifically designed to work specific groups of muscles. Therefore, there are weight machines for abdominals, **lats**, pectorals, and thigh muscles, along with many others. A weight machine usually features a stack of weights, though some use systems of hydraulic resistance instead. For weight-stack machines, you select the weight you want to lift, pull, or push by putting a pin into a notch on the side of the stack. Weights machines can be extremely advanced, including ones that alter the resistance according to how tired your muscles become as you go through a **set** of **reps**. Other advantages include:

- They usually feature more weight options than free weights, so you can pick the level at which you want to train.
- They are safer to use because they are designed to hold you securely while training. You can usually lift more because you do not have to worry about balance.
- You will not need a **spotter**—if you are having problems lifting a weight, the machine will let you lower it safely to rest.

If you are trying to decide between weight machines and freeweights, then don't—use both. Combining the two ensures a well-rounded physique and an endless variety of exercises. The biggest question is where you will train.

A "spotter" stands over a person who is weight training to provide assistance and monitor safety. Bench press exercises such as this always require a spotter in case the weight is dropped.

SAFE TRAINING

Weight training can be done at home or in a local gym. Home training is very convenient—you can train whenever you want to, without having to travel. However, for someone new to weight training, the disadvantages of training at home outweigh the advantages.

Home training is often done unsupervised, so there is a greater danger of injuring yourself by using poor technique or the wrong type of equipment, or by lifting weights that are too heavy for you. Also, you have the expense of setting up a home gym. Simple freeweights can be bought relatively inexpensively, but add on the weight bench and you might spend $200. A complete weight machine center will easily cost you $800–1,000. Another disadvantage is that people who train at home are more likely to give up. Exercising at home can be lonely, and does not provide the motivation that comes from training around large groups of people.

Using a school or private gym solves these problems. A modern, well-equipped gym will contain a mix of both freeweights and weight machines in large

BODYBUILDING HISTORY

Weight training as we know it today originated in the late nineteenth century. Gyms spread throughout Europe and the United States, and by the 1930s, bodybuilding competitions were being held. These gave bodybuilders the opportunity to show off their bodies, and in 1939 the first Mr. America competition was held under the auspices of the Amateur Athletic Union. Competitive bodybuilding went international in 1946 when Ben and Joe Weider—whose surname is often seen on weights and weight equipment—formed the International Federation of Body Building (IFBB). The IFBB promoted the art of bodybuilding in world competitions, including the prestigious Mr. Olympia and Mrs. Olympia. Bodybuilding is not yet an Olympic event, although the International Olympic Committee is becoming more accepting of the sport.

The world-famous weightlifter Yuri Vlasov (from the former Soviet Union) is seen here hoisting a massive stack of weights. Vlasov has held Olympic, World, and European titles.

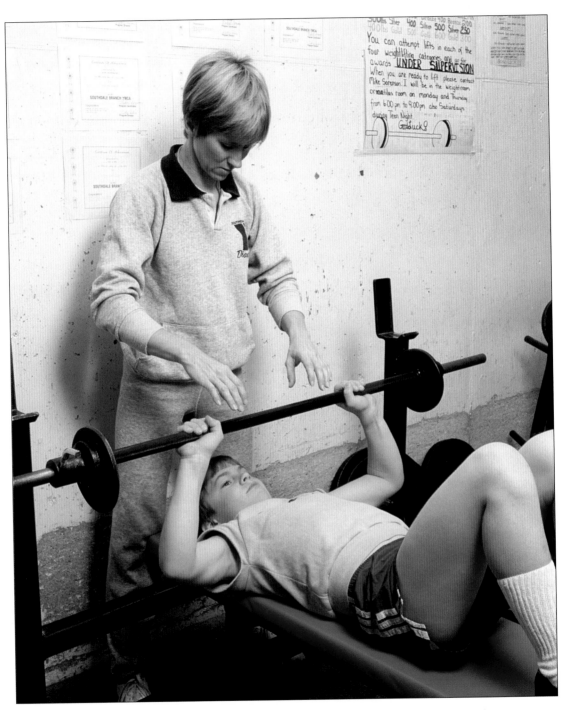

Always learn weight training through a qualified instructor. The major cause of weightlifting injury is poor technique, often combined with a sudden increase in attempted weight.

numbers. There will also be experts within the gym to advise on safe and effective technique. Most gyms will make you go through a short introductory course to teach you the fundamentals of how to use the equipment. Some schools and colleges have gyms that are free of charge to students.

Whether you choose to exercise at home or in a local gym, weight training is an excellent discipline to get you fit and in shape. "Discipline," however, is an important word. Your mind must be as fit and controlled as your body in order to get the most out of weight training, as we will see in the next chapter.

JOINING A GYM

Look inside a gym before you join. The quality of its staff, equipment, and surroundings has an impact on your safety when training, so check the following points:

- **Is the gym clean and well kept? Remember to also look in the showers and changing areas.**
- **Are all the pieces of gym equipment in good condition? Are freeweights stacked in order of weight? Look out, too, for things such as torn seating or frayed cables on the weight machines.**
- **Is the gym using weight machines made by reputable brands, such as Bodymaster or Nautilus? If you are not familiar with the names, ask a sports professional (such as an assistant in a professional sports shop) about them.**
- **Are the freeweights free of rust?**
- **Is the atmosphere inside the gym friendly but disciplined?**

A Strong Mind

Weight training is an activity requiring mental, as much as physical, discipline. One of the biggest challenges is to develop your strength gradually and safely, even when you are eager to push ahead more quickly.

Injuries occur in weight training mainly because of careless technique or overly ambitious weight loading. Impatience is often the reason for this. Weight training has a rhythm to it. During the first six weeks of training—if you train regularly and properly—improvements to your physique can be quite rapid. Muscles in the arms, chest, and shoulders will tone up and strengthen, and you may find you lose some weight. After this period, however, progress becomes much slower. As your body strengthens, you will need to work harder to develop the muscles further.

When you struggle to put on more muscle, several things can happen. First, you may simply become discouraged and stop training. To counter this, focus on the improvements to your fitness rather than the improvements to your appearance. However much you develop your muscles, there will always be someone bigger, more toned, and (at least in your eyes) more attractive. If your only reason for doing weight training is to look good, ask yourself whether there is a deeper reason. Do you want people to respect you more? Do you want more attention from the opposite sex? You may have a poor self-image. Work out what it is you really want; simply putting on muscle bulk is unlikely to solve problems with self-image. Concentrate on the

However hard it is to lift a weight, do not hold your breath under the tension. This deprives muscles of oxygen and makes them more likely to be damaged.

Weight training should build a disciplined mind. Set goals for every session, and always concentrate on using correct technique rather than lifting huge weights.

improvements in how you feel rather than on how you look. Enjoy the fact that you are getting fitter and stronger, and treat improvements in appearance as a bonus.

Of course, the other reason you might stop training is boredom. Weight training can be very repetitive, and if you are not seeing big muscle gain, the inclination to stop training can be high. There are several things you can do to stop weight training from becoming boring:

- Vary your routines at the gym. If you concentrate on doing upper-body workouts one day, switch the next day to lower-body workouts, or spend more time on the **cardiovascular** machines.

- Shorten your workouts on some days. After a proper warm-up, you can do weights for just fifteen minutes and still get the benefit. In that time, you can do several exercises to work your legs, lats, **pecs**, **traps**, **delts**, and abdominals. Short routines are not for every time you go to the gym, but just for now and then, on those days when you really want to be somewhere else.
- Plan an enjoyable activity with your training partner for after the weights session. Following training with something exciting has the effect of making the training itself more exciting.

STEADY TRAINING

Weight training cannot be rushed. Do not be tempted to make large jumps in the weights you are using. Adding 10 pounds (4.5 kg) to your weight stack when you are already struggling is a recipe for torn muscles, **ligaments**, and **tendons**. It can even result in a **stroke** caused by an **aneurysm**. Furthermore, do not overtrain by visiting the gym too often. During weight training, muscle fibers suffer microscopic tears from the effort. The fibers heal themselves in stronger configurations during periods of rest. If you do not have at least one day of rest between training days, this healing and muscle development cannot take place. Therefore, your muscles will be vulnerable to injury during training.

For people under the age of eighteen, there are some clear rules to training. Do not train more than three times a week, and keep training sessions under forty-five minutes—ideally, closer to thirty minutes. When you first start on a particular machine or freeweights exercise, practice the technique lifting no weight at all. Then lift weights under expert supervision until you can demonstrate perfect technique in up to fifteen repetitions. According to sports medicine experts Avery Faigenbaum and Wayne Westcott, the young weightlifter should add weights in increments of 1–3 pounds (0.5–1.5 kg) and perform one to three sets at the new weight. Once they can demonstrate perfect technique at the new weight, they may add further weights.

Another important ingredient for safe training is concentration. Whenever you lift, pull, or push a weight, focus all your attention on the muscle groups doing the work. If, for instance, you are doing a **biceps** curl exercise on a machine, concentrate on the slow curling action of your arms up toward your chest and the release back down to the starting position. Feel what the muscles are doing throughout the lift, and move only your forearms—the rest of your body should be entirely still. To aid your concentration, synchronize your breathing with the action. Do not hold your breath (which is a common mistake) because this deprives the muscles of the vital oxygen they need to work. Breathe out as you lift the weights to your chest, and inhale as you lower them. Maintaining concentration throughout a lift helps to protect you from injuries caused by poor technique.

Don't judge yourself by others' physiques. Huge arm muscles such as these should only be seen in adults, as they are only achieved through lifting extremely heavy weights.

EXERCISE FOR IMPROVING CONCENTRATION

Use eye focus to maintain concentration. Notice that throughout this lift, the woman keeps her eyes focused forward on some point in the distance. This keeps attention from wandering and aids in maintaining good body posture.

Sit in front of a small object you have seen many times before, such as a pen or spoon, placed on a table. Make sure you are comfortable, and keep a watch or clock within view. Breathe slowly and stare at the object, examining it closely. Try to notice every detail: color, shape, texture, any damage, and so on. Your aim is to see things you have not noticed before. Do not let your concentration wander—keep looking. All of a sudden, you will see the object as if you are looking at it for the very first time—at least, that's the goal.

Practice for only five minutes at first. Next time, practice for ten minutes. Increase the time limit as far as your daily schedule will allow. If you can spend twenty to thirty minutes doing this, you will develop the right powers of concentration for your weight training.

Preparing the Body

Before each session of weight training, you have to prepare the body in order to reduce the risks of injury. Do this in two stages: warming up and stretching.

Many people arrive in a gym and rush straight to their favorite weight machine, lifting as much as they can. They are heading for the doctor. Weight training with cold and stiff muscles is a recipe for quick injury, mainly sprains and strains. Doing a proper warm-up routine will prepare your body for training, which in turn means that each weight session will bring more progress.

WARMING UP

A warm-up routine does exactly what it says—it warms up the muscles, ligaments, and tendons of the body in preparation for exercise. A warm muscle is more pliable and flexible than a cold muscle, which means that you can put it through an extended range of movement without damaging it. Muscles also rely on oxygen to give them energy to work. Oxygen is carried to the muscles in the blood, and the blood picks up the oxygen as it passes through the lungs. During a warm-up routine, both breathing and heart-rate are increased by light exercise. The overall effect is that we breathe in more air, more oxygen is delivered to the blood, and the blood is pumped faster around the body.

A basic warm-up routine involves light exercise for between five and ten

Begin any weight session with light, manageable weights. Light dumbbells can be used as part of your warm-up to increase the muscle temperature of the arms and shoulders.

This stretch works to loosen the hamstrings, knee tendons, and calves. If you cannot touch your toes, try to at least touch your ankles.

minutes, just enough to get slightly out of breath, raise the heartbeat, and warm the muscles. The key rule of a warm-up is not to do anything too strenuous, but merely to prepare the muscles for exercise. Here is a typical warm-up routine:

1. Run very lightly on the spot without raising your knees too high. Shake your arms loosely by your sides to get rid of any stiffness in the arms and shoulders. Run for about two to three minutes, slightly increasing the pace and the height you raise the knees.

2. Stand up straight with your legs shoulder-width apart, looking straight ahead. Swing your arms forward in large circles about ten times, then reverse the direction of the circles. Finally, swing the arms inward across your chest so that they cross each other, then outward again. Repeat ten times. This will warm up your shoulders.

3. To warm up your neck muscles, make large circles with your head in one direction about five times. Then reverse the direction for another five times. Brush the chest with your chin at the lowest point of the circle and stretch your head up rather than back at the top of the circle.

4. To warm up the leg and knee muscles, do about two minutes of lunges— stepping forward and then back with one leg, and repeating with the other. Do not push too hard, and make sure you bend the thigh so that it is at about forty-five degrees to the floor.

5. Make large circles with your hips, first in one direction and then in the other. The circles should be as wide as possible, with your hands placed on your hips to facilitate the movement.

6. Finally, shake your entire body to loosen up and complete the warm-up.

This warm-up does not use machines. However, in a gym you can warm up on some of the special aerobic machines. The rowing machine, treadmill, stepper, and track machine (which imitates a skiing action) are all suitable. Try to combine two machines with different actions so that you warm up your entire body. A good combination would be the rowing machine and the

Lunges are good warm-up exercises. Bend the thigh until it is parallel to the floor, but keep the back upright at all times (keeping your hands behind your head will help you to do this).

STRETCHING RULES

If stretching is performed improperly, it will do more harm than good. Here are some key rules to make stretching safe and effective:

- **Do not bounce or jerk for a deeper stretch. Using your body weight in this way to push yourself further often results in torn ligaments and muscles.**
- **Keep breathing deeply throughout the stretch. The breathing ensures that the muscles are kept supplied with vital oxygen.**
- **Stop the stretch immediately if you experience any sharp or burning pains.**
- **Relax into a stretch. Do not tense the muscles because this tightens them and makes them more prone to injury.**

stepper. Whatever machine you use, start at a gentle pace and work only hard enough to raise your breathing and temperature.

Once you have finished your warm-up, you can proceed to stretching.

STRETCHING

Flexibility is essential for almost every sport, including weight training. A weight training session should work all the major muscle groups of the body, so your flexibility preparation must do the same. There are a huge number of different stretches you can do. Ask a qualified sports coach, yoga teacher, or similar flexibility expert to teach you a broad repertoire of techniques. Organize these into a specific routine that you will use before every weight-training session. Work from your feet to your head, or vice versa, so that you do not miss any important muscles. Importantly, avoid stretching any injured muscles or ligaments until they are fully healed.

Here is a basic stretching routine:

1. **Seated hamstring stretch**—sit on the floor with your legs stretched out in front of you and your back straight. Breathe in and bend forward from the waist until you can grip your ankles. Holding onto your ankles, bend farther forward until you can feel a stretch along the calf muscles and the back of the knee. Hold the position before about ten seconds and then sit up slowly.

2. **Quadriceps stretch**—stand up straight, resting one hand against a wall for stability. Lift up your left leg behind you, then take hold of the top of the foot with your left hand and pull the heel up toward your buttocks. You should feel the stretch along the front of the thigh and the knee. Hold the position for about thirty seconds, then let go of the foot and return to the floor. Repeat this exercise with your right leg.

3. **Groin stretch**—sit on the floor and draw your feet into the groin, pressing the soles of the feet together so that the knees fall outward.
   Take hold of your ankles with your hands, and push down on the knees using your elbows. The stretch is concentrated along the inside of the groin. Hold the stretch for about twenty seconds,

The seated hamstring stretch. Stop stretching immediately if you feel any sudden increase in heat or pain at the back of the knee.

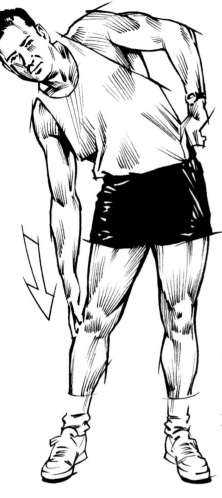

Side stretches will increase the flexibility of your stomach muscles and loosen the torso in preparation for weight training.

then gently release the pressure on your knees and bring them up to the center.

4. **Side stretch**—stand with your legs in an "A"-shape two shoulder-widths apart. Keeping your back straight, slide your left hand down the side of your left leg as far as you can. Once you have reached your maximum position, hold it for five seconds, then slowly come up again to the middle. Then repeat the exercise on the right side. Repeat the set three times.

5. **Waist and back stretch**—again, stand with your legs in an "A"-shape two shoulder-widths apart. Bend straight forward from the waist and lower your torso as far as it will go, keeping your back straight. Holding the legs and gently pulling on them will help you to go down farther. Hold the stretch for about ten seconds, then move your body upright again. Place your hands against your lower back and stretch your body backward, looking up at the ceiling as you do. Hold for ten seconds, then release.

6. **Shoulder stretch**—hold your left arm straight out in front of you and hook your right forearm around the back of the left elbow. Keeping the left arm straight, use the right arm to pull it across your body until you feel a strong stretch in the shoulder joint. Hold for ten seconds, then release and switch arms.

7. **Neck stretch**—standing up straight, lower your chin so that it rests against your chest. You should feel a stretch up the back of your neck. Hold for five seconds, then release. Next, bend your head backward and look up toward the ceiling. Do not let your head fall too far backward because this can damage your top vertebrae. Instead, feel you are stretching your face up toward the ceiling. Hold for five seconds and release. Finally, twist your head to look left and then right, each time holding the stretch for five seconds.

MEDICAL QUESTIONNAIRE

If you answer yes to any of the following questions, you should have a medical checkup before beginning any program of weight training.

- **Have you ever suffered from any sort of heart condition that has stopped you from doing physical exercise?**
- **Do you suffer from asthma?**
- **Are you on any medication for an existing illness?**
- **Have you ever suffered serious injury or illness affecting your spine, neck, bones, or certain body joints?**
- **Have you ever experienced any chest pains during physical activity?**
- **Do you suffer from periods of dizziness or fainting?**
- **Do you have epilepsy or any other condition that results in seizures or loss of consciousness?**
- **Do you have any other medical condition that might affect your ability to do physical exercise?**

Safe Weight Training

A large percentage of weight-training injuries come from misuse of equipment and the wrong type of training. For anyone younger than eighteen, incorrect technique or weight selection can have a very harmful long-term effect on the growing body.

Many people frown on the idea of weight training for people under the age of eighteen. The main concern is that loading the still-growing body with heavy weights can deform and damage it, leaving the young person with injuries that last a lifetime.

Young people have several important physiological differences from adults, all of which relate to the process of growing. First, during periods of growth, muscles and **cartilage** are at an increased risk of injury as they stretch to cope with the lengthening of the body. Second, growth makes body joints more unstable because muscles around the joints are also adjusting to growth. Finally, the skeleton itself is stretching. In the long bones of the body (such as those that are found in the legs and arms), there are "growth plates," special sections of the bone which enable it to lengthen properly. Loading the growing bones with excessive weight can deform these growth plates and lead to permanent bone damage. Similarly, the growing spine is vulnerable to injury and distortion under heavy weights.

An instructor provides guidance on correct dumbbell technique. Avoid any jerking movements, and try to move only those muscles (in this case, the biceps) which are meant to be working.

Though these cautions are extremely important, they do not mean that you should never do weight training. Safe weight training for those under eighteen is a matter of learning the correct technique and avoiding dangerous exercises.

THE RIGHT ROUTINE

For young people, the recommended frequency of weight training is two to three sessions per week. Two is the ideal number because it lets you do other forms of exercise. Mixing weight training with sports such as running, swimming, and basketball is also recommended because cross-training provides an all-round level of fitness, which helps guard against injury. Doing only weight training may be too hard on your bones, joints, and muscles.

Adult bodybuilders will attempt to lift the heaviest weights possible as part of their routines. Do not attempt to do this if you are under eighteen—your body is not yet strong enough to support extremely concentrated weight stacks. Gauge the right level of weight for you by the number of repetitions. If you cannot lift, pull, or push a weight with proper technique for eight consecutive repetitions, it is too heavy for you. Instead of aiming to lift large weights, focus on increasing the number of repetitions you do with a weight you can lift comfortably, two sets per exercise.

Steer clear of dead lifts. Dead lifts involve lifting a heavy barbell weight without using a bench, seat, or other support to stabilize you. Your body will undergo dangerous stress during a dead lift, as different muscles throughout the body attempt to keep their balance under the sudden weight.

Never be tempted to insert the pin far down the weight stack just to see if you can lift a heavy weight. Work progressively. Start with the first weight on the stack, and move down gradually.

All weight training should be done slowly and methodically. When lifting, never snatch or jerk the weight. Instead, move it steadily from the start position to the stop position, and always go through the full range of body motion for the exercise. This is where good technique makes a difference.

GOOD TECHNIQUE

Do not use any machine or attempt any new freeweight lift until an expert has coached you in it. Freeweights are especially dangerous. Not only are more muscles required for balance when lifting a freeweight, but incorrect technique may result in dropping the weight on yourself as well. This last danger is one reason why you should always have a spotter with you when attempt freeweight lifting.

There are some basic principles of technique applicable to almost all weight-training exercises. These involve how we stand, sit, bend, and breathe. Posture is extremely important in weight training. For example, if we sit in a slouching position while performing an overhead press exercise, the spine is placed under unnatural pressure, like a stick

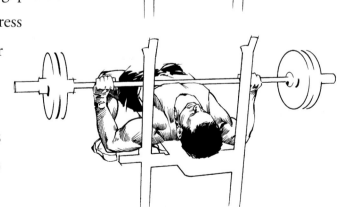

During a bench press, support the back muscles by keeping feet flat and the back straight — do not arch the back during the exercise.

being bent until it snaps. If we sit straight, however, the vertebrae of the spine distribute the pressure evenly and naturally. To achieve the proper sitting position, push your buttocks to the very back of the seat and keep your back straight. Lift your chin up, and pull your shoulders back to avoid slouching. Your feet must be flat on the floor and slightly back toward your thighs.

Note that the correct upper-body sitting position is also the correct upper-body standing and bending position. Learning how to sit and stand properly is valuable because it affects how we handle weights safely. For example, a popular weight training exercise is the barbell squat. Here a barbell is held

Lighter weights may not build up huge muscle volume, but used in high repetitions they tone and shape muscles to produce a fit and athletic physique.

behind the neck and across the shoulders, using an overhand grip. With the weight in this position, the quadriceps, hamstrings, and **gluteals** are exercised by slowly bending the knees until the thighs are parallel to the floor, and then slowly returning to the start position. During this exercise, the back needs to be kept as upright as possible, with the head up and face looking forward; otherwise, the spine will take the pressure of the exercise rather than the leg muscles.

Bending to pick up or handle any weight must be done from the legs and not the back. Try this exercise: place any object (it need not be a heavy one) on the floor. Stand with your feet close to it and your back straight. Look directly forward. Now bend from your knees and lower yourself down beside the object. At the same time, keep your back as straight up as possible. Once you have taken hold of the object, lift your face and look straight forward—this helps to keep your back upright. Complete the lift by using your legs to push the weight from the floor. If the weight is heavy, keep it close to your stomach, the body's natural center of gravity.

Protecting your back will save you many problems if you are going to take weight training seriously. Get into the habit of sitting, standing, and bending properly at all times, and these habits will be transferred into the gym.

GOOD BREATHING

Correct breathing is as much a part of good technique as correct posture. Strong breathing maintains the supply of oxygen to the muscles while they are working. The problem with the way that many of us breathe is that we do not use the full capacity of our lungs, resulting in a poor input of oxygen. Worse still, while exerting ourselves as in weight training, we have the tendency to hold our breath. This is positively dangerous in weight training because the combination of held breath and muscular exertion can actually result in a stroke, as the oxygen to the brain is cut off.

It is very important that you learn proper full-lung breathing. Draw in a deep breath through your nose. Imagine that you are pulling the breath down into your stomach; you will notice that your abdomen inflates first, followed by your chest. This sequence indicates that the whole of the lung from bottom to top is filled with air. Exhale from your mouth; the chest will collapse first, followed by the stomach.

HANDLING EQUIPMENT SAFELY

Setting up a machine or handling freeweights properly is the first step in safe technique. Here are a few key points to remember:

- Make sure that pins are properly engaged in the weight stacks.

- Adjust the whole piece of equipment to your personal body dimensions. If equipment is set too long or too short for you, this will put unnatural pressure on certain joints and cause you to lose correct body posture.

- While exercising, keep your hands, legs, and clothing away from any chains, pulleys, belts, or moving parts. Also, keep your hands and feet away from the weight stacks when they are moving.

- Before using any equipment, check it for loose parts, frayed cables, bent pins, or other signs of damage.

The danger point of seated pull-downs is often during the release of the weight. Keep it under control, and never be tempted to just let go of the bar. Also make sure that the handgrips are not sweaty.

When using a weights bench, keep the small of the back pressed down onto the flat surface. A good way to do this is by raising the knees and putting the feet flat on the bench.

Use deep breathing throughout your weight training. However, make sure you follow a specific rhythm. When you lift, pull, or push the weight (known as the "power phase"), breathe out. When you relax the weight back to its starting position, breathe in. This sequence keeps you from holding your breath. The power phase of any exercise should take three full seconds to complete, as should the return phase. Count this rhythm mentally by saying, "one elephant, two elephants, three elephants." Using the word "elephant" ensures that you count in complete seconds. Counting in this way also prevents you from using those rapid, jerky movements which are so apt to result in injury.

GYM ETIQUETTE AND PERSONAL SAFETY

- Do not wear jewelry when weight training, particularly necklaces, rings, and earrings. As well as being a hazard to you, some jewelry—especially rings—can scratch or damage the handles of equipment.

- Do not wear excessively baggy T-shirts, which can get caught in machinery. If you are using the rowing machine, tuck your T-shirt into the waistband of your shorts or gym trousers to prevent them from getting caught in the runners.

- If using freeweights, place them back on the freeweights rack in the same order in which they were arranged. If you have added weights to a bar, it is polite to remove them after use.

- Never leave any litter in the gym, and make sure all bags and personal belongings are safely out of the way.

- When using weight machines, wear good quality training shoes with rubber nonskid soles to prevent slipping.

Gym clothing should be light and comfortable. If training shoes have long laces, tuck the loose ends away to keep them from being caught in machinery.

Treating Common Injuries

Weight training can have many positive health effects. It aids back problems, weak bones, asthma, and injured knees, as well as other complaints. Yet weight training also carries the risk of muscle and joint damage if practiced improperly.

Avoid weights that are too heavy, obey the rules of good technique, and develop **antagonistic muscles**, and you will go a long way toward preventing injury. Even so, regular weight training is capable of imposing wear and tear on all the joints and muscles. Treating such injuries is a matter of letting the injuries heal naturally, then strengthening the injured part to withstand further exercise.

SPRAINS AND STRAINS

Sprains and strains are the most common injuries encountered during weight training. A sprain occurs when ligaments in a joint are torn, either by an unnatural range of movement (such as when you twist your ankle) or by a combination of extreme pressure and twisting. Strains refer to muscle pain caused by overwork or overstretching.

Sprains and strains account for the vast majority of injuries incurred in weight training. These are usually caused by lifting excessive weight or by poor technique,

When the body is placed under extreme tension, the biggest danger is the sudden rupture of muscles and tendons. This usually occurs when using weights at the limit of one's capability.

OVERUSE INJURIES

An overuse, or chronic, injury is caused by repeating the same action many times. This is not as serious as an acute injury, but any chronic problem may become worse if not acknowledged early on, so weight lifters should seek medical advice and treatment. Overuse injuries have both mental and physical symptoms:

- unusual tiredness or fatigue
- a lack of appetite
- an inability to sleep at night
- muscle soreness and cramps
- stiff, painful, or unstable joints
- problems getting parts of the body comfortable in bed at night
- painful tendons
- pain that shows no improvement after three days

particularly if you lose your balance during freeweights exercise. The following are the telltale symptoms:

- significant pain in a joint or muscle;
- restricted mobility in a joint or limb;
- swelling or redness around the injury;
- a feeling of weakness in a limb at certain ranges of its movement;
- trouble getting the injured area comfortable at night;
- lack of strength in an injured limb.

Fortunately, the vast majority of sprains and strains can be treated without the help of a doctor. The initial stages of self-treatment can be remembered by thinking of the word "P.R.I.C.E.," which stands for Protection, Rest, Ice, Compression, and Elevation:

Protection

If you are injured, stop training immediately, and protect the injured area from further damage by restricting all unnecessary activity. If, for example, you have sprained your shoulder, avoid exercises such as bench presses, dumbbell flyes, or pec workouts.

Rest

Give the injured area complete rest for at least a week. This does not necessarily mean that you have to stop training. An injured knee need not prevent you from doing upper-body training on seated weight machines. Make sure that whatever training you continue to do, no further strain is placed on the injured part. Restrict other activities and sports that affect the injury.

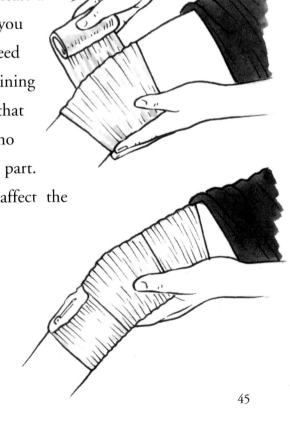

A damaged knee or elbow joint can be protected by using elastic bandage. Wrap the bandage around the joint so that it extends above and below it. Finally, secure it in place with fastening clips.

MUSCLES OF THE SHOULDER AND BACK

The diagram below displays the main muscle groups of the back and the effect if the particular muscle is damaged by injury.

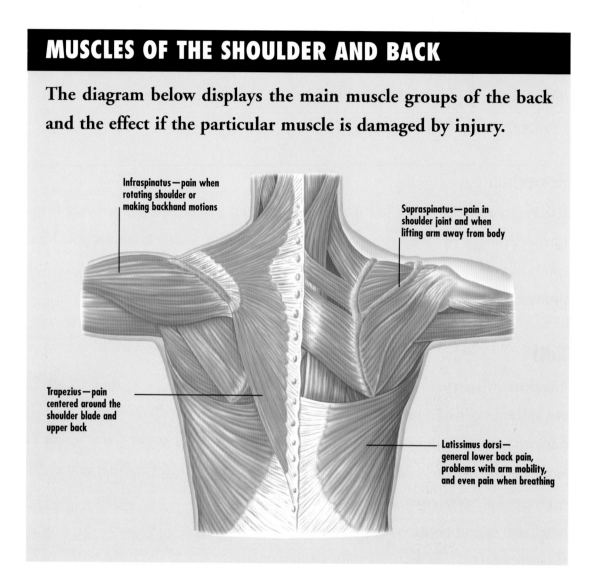

Infraspinatus—pain when rotating shoulder or making backhand motions

Supraspinatus—pain in shoulder joint and when lifting arm away from body

Trapezius—pain centered around the shoulder blade and upper back

Latissimus dorsi—general lower back pain, problems with arm mobility, and even pain when breathing

Ice

Reduce any swelling around the injury by applying ice packs about two or three times a day, for no longer than twenty minutes each time. If there is no swelling, you might find it more beneficial to apply heat treatments. Heat-generating ointments are available from sports shops and drug stores, and they are particularly useful for reducing pain in muscle strains. Do not use heat treatments on swelling areas.

Compression

Wrap the injury firmly in an elastic bandage or, ideally, a professional compression bandage. Applying strong support to a strain or sprain reduces swelling and also protects the joint or muscle against further damage.

Elevation

Elevate an injured limb on a surface such as a chair or table that is well-padded with cushions. If your leg is injured, try to raise it higher than the hips; and if the arm is injured, position your hand higher than the shoulder. Elevation reduces the amount of blood flowing into a limb, which in turn helps reduce swelling.

SEVERE DAMAGE

If a sprain or strain is fairly slight, P.R.I.C.E. alone will usually cure it within a week. For more severe damage, however, there are two other stages of rehabilitation. Once the pain has subsided and you feel mobility returning to the joint or limb, it is time to introduce what are known as range of motion (**R.O.M.**) exercises. These are light stretching and flexibility exercises meant to give the joint or limb its full range of movement. The stretches used should be gentle, but should explore every direction of movement you had before the accident.

Once you have full, pain-free R.O.M., you need to strengthen the injured joint or muscle. Fortunately, doing weight training means that you will already know exercises to strengthen the injured part of the body. Here again, the key point is that you do all exercises gently. Use very light weights of 1–3 pounds (0.5–1.5 kg), with no strenuous or rapid movements. Build the weight up gradually over a period of several days until you are back to normal levels. Stop training or reduce the weights used if the pain returns.

Treating an injury

To see how the P.R.I.C.E., R.O.M., and strengthening procedure might work for an actual weight-training injury, let us consider how to treat a shoulder injury. Weight training imposes particularly heavy strains upon the shoulders. In many upper-body weight-training exercises, the shoulders are required to make powerful lifts, which puts considerable stress on the shoulder joint and surrounding muscles. A common injury is a damaged **rotator cuff**. The rotator cuff is a group of muscles and ligaments holding the shoulder's ball-and-socket joint together and controlling the arm's rotational movement. About seventy-five percent of shoulder injuries in weight training are caused by damage to the rotator cuff.

The first stage in treatment is to give the joint complete rest. Stop doing any upper-body weight-training exercises that use the injured shoulder, even with light weights. Keep arm activity to a minimum until the pain in the shoulder has subsided. This may take about a week.

R.O.M. exercises

Now it is time for R.O.M. exercises. One particularly good R.O.M. exercise for the shoulder is called "the pendulum:"

1. Stand up and bend over from the waist, supporting yourself by putting a hand against the wall or on a table or other stable object (use the arm on the uninjured side).

2. Hang the arm on the injured side straight downward like a pendulum. Relax the shoulder muscles.

3. Make gentle swinging motions with the arm, forward and back, side to side, and in circles. Change the direction of the swing after about twenty times of using each pattern, and also the direction of the circles.

The pendulum will help free up a stiff shoulder and will also relax damaged muscles. If the pendulum causes no pain, do as many different shoulder stretches as you can design. The only rule is that you do not put any strain or force on the shoulder.

For strength training, a single dumbbell about 2 lbs 3 oz (1 kg) in weight is an ideal piece of equipment. For the shoulder, try the following exercises:

- Hold the dumbbell to the side of the body, then raise your arm straight out to the side until it is at shoulder height (fig A). The thumb should be pointing downward. Hold for three seconds, then gently lower. Repeat two more times.
- Hold the dumbbell to the side of the body, then swing it forward with a straight arm so that the weight is level with your shoulder (fig B). Hold for three seconds and gently lower, then repeat.

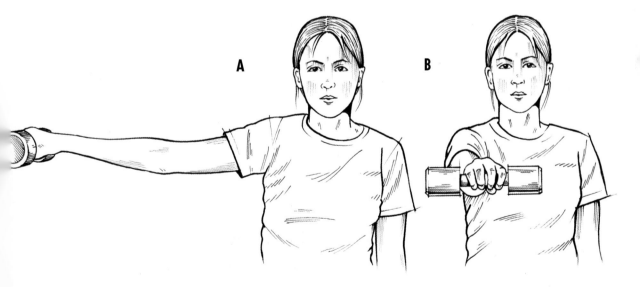

Lifting your arm straight out to the side and to the front while holding a light dumbbell can gradually improve strength when recovering from a minor shoulder injury.

Most strains and sprains are healed by following the above principles or by adapting them to the particular injury. You should always consult a doctor if your efforts do not work. Signs that you need professional help include chronic pain; a limb or joint freezing up or losing mobility, despite flexibility exercises; tingling sensations or numbness in the hands or toes; headaches; and nausea or fatigue following the injury.

TORSO INJURIES

If you are practicing lifting heavy weights, the other danger you might face is injury to the abdomen and back. During a heavy lift, the muscles of these two areas are placed under tremendous strain. Sometimes the strain is too much and the muscles rupture. The first sign of ruptured abdominal muscles is usually a sharp and violent pain in the abdomen at the moment of making a heavy lift. The stomach becomes painful to the touch, and any activity that uses the abdominal muscles, even walking, is difficult.

Except in the case of major rupture, a good two weeks of rest will usually be enough to heal the injury. Avoid body positions in which the legs are stretched out straight while lying on your back. This position may increase the tension in the already sensitive muscles. The healing process is aided by the use of heat packs applied to the stomach area; **anti-inflammatory** medicines should help bring down any swelling.

Exercises for the R.O.M. stage of healing are basic:

1. Stand straight up with your feet shoulder-width apart. Then gently run your left hand down the side of your left thigh, stretching the torso over to the side. Repeat on the right side. Do this set of exercises about three times.

2. Place your hands on either side of your spine in the small of your back. Lean the upper body gently backward while looking upward at the ceiling. As your

ABDOMEN

The abdomen is one of the areas most weightlifters concentrate on developing. There are several different muscle groups involved.

Serratus anterior muscle—responsible for drawing the shoulder blade forward when making outward movements with the arm

Internal oblique abdominal muscle—a wide muscle which helps to support the abdominal contents

Rectus abdominis muscles—the muscles running down the center of the abdomen which form a "six pack" when developed

body arches, the abdominal muscles are stretched.

Practice these exercises for two weeks, then gradually introduce very light abdominal weight training. As with any injury, consult a doctor if the pain does not go away or is particularly acute.

Back injuries are similar in many ways to abdominal injuries. At a moment of

BACK MUSCLES

The back is probably the most commonly damaged part of the body in weight training. The diagram shows the important muscle groups which can be affected.

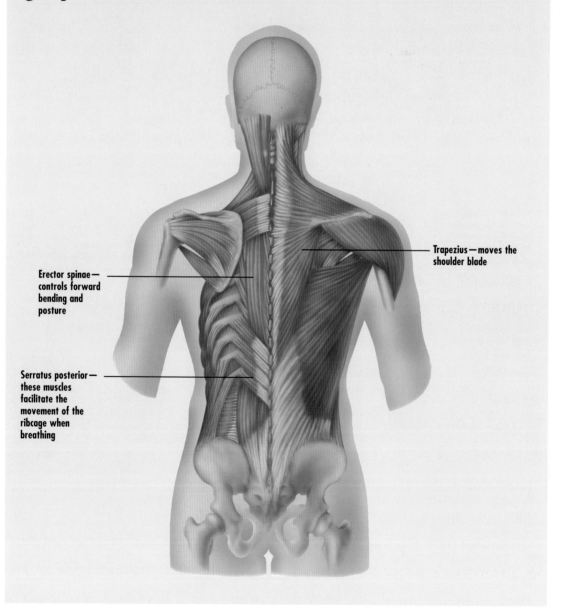

Trapezius—moves the shoulder blade

Erector spinae—controls forward bending and posture

Serratus posterior—these muscles facilitate the movement of the ribcage when breathing

ACHES AND PAINS

Do not treat every ache and pain that follows weight training as an injury. Any sport may result in a phenomenon known as delayed onset muscle soreness (D.O.M.S.). D.O.M.S. happens one or two days after strenuous exercise and is caused by the healing of those tiny tears in the muscle tissue that were incurred during training. Usually the ache will disappear within forty-eight hours. However, if it persists for more than three days, you should see a doctor.

Remember to drink plenty of water before, during, and after your weight training session. This will help muscles lose their soreness after exercise because they will rehydrate quicker.

strain or twisting, pain will shoot through the back muscles. The pain is made worse through movement or lifting, and the back and neck become stiff and difficult to move. Again, the usual course of treatment is rest, aided by heat treatments and painkilling and anti-inflammatory medication (prescribed by either your drugstore or doctor).

As the initial strain becomes bearable, introduce light exercise to increase the back's flexibility and strength. For about a week, do gentle stretches of exactly the same type described for abdominal injuries. Next, do light warm-up routines and undemanding stomach crunches to strengthen the back muscles.

Consult a doctor immediately if you are in any doubt or have other symptoms such as nausea, dizziness, or blood in your urine. In short, treat abdominal or back injuries yourself only if the pain is manageable, you retain some degree of movement,

Professional Weight Sports

There are three main options for someone who wants to turn weight training into a competitive sport: weightlifting, powerlifting, and bodybuilding.

Bodybuilding became popular as a sport in the United States in the 1930s, and has since grown into a massive international competitive activity, as well as a multi-million dollar industry. Both men and women practice the sport, many dreaming of becoming Mr. or Ms. Olympia, the supreme title in all bodybuilding.

A bodybuilding competition lets athletes demonstrate their muscle development in front of a panel of judges. In international competitions, under the International Federation of Body Building (IFBB), there are nine judges. Each competitor must perform a series of "mandatory poses"—in other words, poses that they must display. There are seven mandatory poses for men and five for women. The poses are designed to display the six main muscle groups of the human body: arms, chest, abdomen, shoulders, back, and legs. The bodybuilding is judged and scored according to four qualities: muscle definition, muscle density, muscle mass, and balanced muscular development.

Bodybuilding competitions are as much about art as about strength. Men are obliged to shave their bodies of any hair concealing the muscles. Tanning

Cheryl Haworth is currently one of the United States' best weightlifters, securing numerous medals in international competitions, including gold in the 2001 Junior World Championships.

Female body building is a controversial but popular aspect of weight training. Here a line of women flex their muscles on the competition stage, demonstrating amazing physical form.

products and oils are also used to highlight the contours of the body. Taking part in bodybuilding competitions requires extraordinary dedication. Several hours of training, for at least three days a week, are essential. Unfortunately, the use of **steroids** is widespread among competitive bodybuilders. More and more bodybuilding organizations are clamping down on steroid use and have introduced drug testing before competitions, but there remains much work to be done. You should avoid competing in competitions where steroid use is prevalent.

The opportunities to take part in bodybuilding competitions are huge. A large number of local, national, and international bodybuilding organizations exist and promote their own competitions. Your club, gym, or coach should be able to point you in the direction of beginners' competitions. If not, any good bodybuilding magazine will provide you with a competition calendar.

WEIGHTLIFTING AND POWERLIFTING

Bodybuilding is about the appearance of the athletes. Weightlifting and powerlifting are about sheer strength. Weightlifting has an ancient history, and became an Olympic sport in 1920. Women have also entered weightlifting. In 1987, the first all-female World Championships was held, and women's weightlifting became an Olympic sport in 2000.

Since 1972, competitive weightlifters compete against one another in two different types of lift, the snatch and the clean-and-jerk:

- The snatch involves lifting a weight straight from the floor to above the head in one movement. As the bar is lifted, the weight lifter drops down into a squatting position under the bar, while locking his arms to support the weights above him. Finally, he pushes himself up from the squatting position to a final standing position and holds the weight for a required length of time before lowering it.
- The clean-and-jerk differs in that the weight lifter first transfers the bar to shoulder height as he moves to the squatting position. This is the "clean" part of the technique. The "jerk" comes when the weight lifter pushes up with his legs and thrusts the weight above his head.

In both cases, the judges are looking for good technique as well as the heaviest weight lifted. Any errors in technique will result in points being deducted.

Weightlifting is not a sport recommended for young people under eighteen years old. The strain it places on the muscles and skeleton is huge. The world's greatest weightlifters can haul over 440 lb. (200 kg.) above their heads, but even

A man demonstrates good form during the barbell squat, a technique used to build up thigh muscles.

weights a quarter of that should not be attempted by the young or the untrained. Weightlifters must also be extremely fit, as well as very strong. During each lift, the heart rate is pushed as high as 200 beats per minute, a dangerous level for those without advanced aerobic fitness.

Powerlifting is a fusion of bodybuilding and weightlifting. It originated in bodybuilding gyms in the 1960s, when bodybuilders began to compete as to who could lift the heaviest weight. Today, powerlifting is an international sport, overseen by the International Powerlifting Federation (IPF). There are three lifts in powerlifting: the bench press, squat, and dead lift.

Like weightlifting, powerlifting is suitable only for adult competitors whose bodies have stopped growing. However, if you're interested in either sport, visit powerlifting or weightlifting websites or magazines for more information about upcoming competitions. Watching competitions can teach you a lot about technique and etiquette, even if you are not training in the sport.

If, when you reach the right age for training, you are still interested in weightlifting or powerlifting, find a good team affiliated with a proper professional body such as U.S.A. Wrestling and the International Powerlifting Federation.

ARNOLD SCHWARZENEGGER

Arnold Schwarzenegger is not only a Hollywood star, but also a legendary bodybuilder. Born in Graz, Austria, in 1947, he was fourteen when he began weight training and only seventeen when he won his first trophy. In 1966, he won the Best Built Man in Europe, Mr. Europe, and the International Powerlifting Championship, although he failed to win his first Mr. Universe title. After designing new techniques to hone his body to perfection, he won the amateur Mr. Universe title in London in 1967, and added the professional title the next year.

Next, he moved to the United States, aiming to become Mr. Olympia. In 1970, he did. Since then, he has pursued a film career, but remains involved with fitness education. A governor on the Council of Physical Fitness in the state of California, he is also an international weight trainer for the Special Olympics. One of Arnold's key messages to young athletes is to avoid drugs and to enjoy a clean, healthy lifestyle.

Bodybuilders Franco Columbu and Arnold Schwarzenegger strike some poses. It took Schwarzenegger twenty years to go from lifting his first weights to winning the Mr. Universe title.

Glossary

Aerobic: Exercise that demands increased oxygen, acquired by speeding up the heart rate and breathing.

Aneurysm: A swelling in the wall of an artery caused by an increase in pressure.

Antagonistic muscles: Muscle groups that work in opposite directions to one another, and so provide the full range of movement in a limb or other body area. A good example is the biceps and triceps in the arms.

Anti-inflammatory: A medication that reduces swelling.

Barbell: A long metal bar on which weights are attached for weight training. It is picked up with a two-handed grip.

Biceps: The large muscles on the inside of the upper arm, which flex the arm and forearm.

Cardiovascular: Any exercise that improves the health of the heart and lungs.

Cartilage: Strong connective tissue found in the body's joints and other structures; children have a higher percentage of cartilage than adults, some of which turns to bone as they grow older.

Crunches: An abdominal exercise involving curling the upper-body off the floor from a lying-down position.

Delts: Short for deltoids, the large triangular muscles which cover the shoulder joint and which are used to lift the arm away from the body.

Dumbbell: A short bar featuring a weight on each end. Used for one-handed weight training exercises.

Endorphins: Any of a group of hormones in the body which produce pain-killing effects and feelings of pleasure and well-being.

Freeweights: Weight-training equipment consisting simply of a bar onto which weights are placed.

Gluteals: Refers to the gluteus muscles in the human buttocks, which are responsible for moving the thigh.

Lats: An abbreviation of "latissimus dorsi," the pair of large triangular muscles covering the lower back.

Ligament: A short band of tough body tissue which connects bones or holds together joints.

Pecs: Short for "pectorals," a muscle group in the chest area.

Reps: Short for "repetitions," the number of times an exercise is repeated.

R.O.M.: Abbreviation for Range of Motion, which may refer to exercises designed to restore full flexibility to a damaged joint or muscle.

Rotator cuff: The group of muscles holding the shoulder joint in place and enabling the rotational movement of the arm.

Set: A complete group of repetitions.

Spotter: The person who assists a gymnast in making a technique during training.

Steroids: A group of chemicals that increase sex hormones in the body, resulting in increased muscular development and strength. However, they can seriously damage health.

Stroke: A potentially life-threatening condition in which the functions of the brain are impaired by a stoppage of blood flow around the brain.

Tendons: A cord of body tissue connecting a muscle to a bone.

Traps: Short for "trapezii," a pair of triangular muscles over the back of the neck and shoulders.

Triceps: The muscles on the back of the upper arm.

Further Information

USEFUL WEB SITES

For news, views, and advice on bodybuilding and weight training, try:

www.muscleandfitness.com

www.thepumpingstation.com

www.wlinfo.com

For general news and articles on powerlifting, see: www.powerlifting.com

U.S.A. Weightlifting: www.usaweightlifting.org

The Web sites listed on this page were active at the time of publication. The publisher is not responsible for Web sites that have changed their address or discontinued operation since the date of publication. The publisher will review and update the Web sites upon each reprint.

FURTHER READING

Cane, Jonathan, with Deidre Johnson-Cane, and Joe Glickman. *The Complete Idiots Guide to Weight Training*. Indianapolis: Alpha Books, 2000.

Delavier, Frederic. *Strength Training Anatomy*. Champaign, Illinois: Human Kinetics, 2001.

Faigenbaum, Avery and Wayne Westcott. *Strength and Power Training for Young Atheletes*. Champaign, Illinois: Human Kinetics, 2000.

Roberts, Oliver. *The Beginner's Guide to Weight Training*. Hauppauge, New York: Barrons Educational Series, 2003.

Schwarzenegger, Arnold and Bill Dobbins. *The New Encyclopedia of Modern Bodybuilding*. London: Fireside, 1999.

THE AUTHOR

Dr. Chris McNab is a writer and editor specializing in sports, survival, and other human-performance topics. He has written more than twenty-five books, and recent publications include *Survival First Aid, Martial Arts for People with Disabilities, Living Off the Land,* and *How to Pass the SAS Selection Course.* Chris lives in South Wales, U.K.

THE CONSULTANTS

Susan Saliba, Ph.D., is a senior associate athletic trainer and a clinical instructor at the University of Virginia in Charlottesville, Virginia. A certified athletic trainer and licensed physical therapist, Dr. Saliba provides sports medicine care, including prevention, treatment, and rehabilitation for the varsity athletes at the University. Dr. Saliba holds dual appointments as an Assistant Professor in the Curry School of Education and the Department of Orthopaedic Surgery. She is a member of the National Athletic Trainers' Association's Educational Executive Committee and its Clinical Education Committee.

Eric Small, M.D., a Harvard-trained sports medicine physician, is a nationally recognized expert in the field of sports injuries, nutritional supplements, and weight management programs. He is author of *Kids & Sports* (2002) and is Assistant Clinical Professor of Pediatrics, Orthopedics, and Rehabilitation Medicine at Mount Sinai School of Medicine in New York. He is also Director of the Sports Medicine Center for Young Athletes at Blythedale Children's Hospital in Valhalla, New York. Dr. Small has served on the American Academy of Pediatrics Committee on Sports Medicine for the past six years, where he develops national policy regarding children's medical issues and sports.

Index

Page numbers in *italics* refer to photographs and illustrations.